DAD Loves Me a lot...

GRIZZLY BEAR series

Author

M Borhan

From

Big 6 Publishing

Sketch of Father Grizzly Bear

In the serene beauty of the forest, the father grizzly bear finds boundless joy in playful moments with its cubs. With a gentle nuzzle, he leads them into the sunlit meadow, where they frolic together in a whirl of fur and laughter. Patiently, he imparts the art of fishing, guiding their eager paws in the rushing river's dance, their tiny reflections mirroring his own. As night falls, the den becomes a sanctuary of warmth and love, where the father grizzly wraps his cubs in a tender embrace, their soft breaths mingling in the stillness. Ever watchful, he stands guard over his precious family, a steadfast protector in the wild expanse.

Amidst shared meals of freshly caught fish and whispered bedtime stories beneath the starlit sky, the bond between father grizzly and cubs grows stronger, a testament to the enduring beauty of family in the heart of nature's embrace.

The father grizzly bear plays a crucial role in the upbringing of its offspring, although its involvement differs from that of the mother. While the mother primarily nurtures and protects the cubs during their early stages of life, the father's presence is often felt through indirect means. Despite this, the presence of dominant male bears in certain territories can indirectly influence the behavior and survival of cubs. Dominant males may establish territories that provide resources and protection, indirectly benefiting the mother and her offspring.

This is the story of my father, my Daddy, who tirelessly works for our family in the woods.
HONEY

My Dad's job is to search, find and locate all the places available for finding the Best Honey in the world...he goes to each place for collecting them.

One day, I was remembering the Old Days
Memories of Daddy with my mother. She told
me how Daddy learned the art of Painting
Only for me in the Tokyo Tour.

Tokyo Tour
While I was a toddler, and I went on a tour with my Dad, we saw A Japanese skilled painter - was making paintings beautifully in a Tokyo Hotel

I was very surprised !! WOW!!
My Dad also stumbled !!
Also, he determined to learn
painting for me!
Tokyo
Tour

Tokyo
Tour
After that, Dad started learning to paint all day
and night, tirelessly to make paintings for me!!

After many weeks of struggle, finally Dad made my painting beautifully!!
Tokyo Tour

After Many Many Days....
Finally, I sent a letter to my Dad, remembering all of these memories. He has been away from home for his work for long, long days now...

Thankfully, Daddy read my letter and decided to come home after a long time, ...so he packed all his belongings before starting for home!

Dad returns Home....
Wow, finally that day arrived! My father has come home after a long, long break, I was rejoicing with my mother, also everyone around us!

At first, Dad hugged my younger toddler brother, who is just 1 year of age. He loved and hugged him for a long time...

After that, Dad gave me a bunch of love, with a
Red Lollipop Candy...

Wow!! I was surprised - Dad also bought for me many more candies, cupcakes and gave me a Full Red Heart !!

I was extremely happy, my father also bought new clothes for me! WOW!!
I ran and hugged my Dad. I jumped onto his lap, and I was in a harmony of signing with joy...

I was more surprised and overwhelmed with joy
when he gave me new toys, gifts and presents
boxes and balloons...

I was really overwhelmed, how my Dad had
brought me Big Boxes of Joy even after many
years he has come back home, he didn't forget
my choices at all...
I realized that how much he loves me...
Yes, Dad Loves me a lot...

www.ingramcontent.com/pod-product-compliance
Lightning Source LLC
Chambersburg PA
CBHW042120150726
48005CB00026B/208